This book belongs to:

For Kit and Ren

First published 2023 by Walker Books Ltd
87 Vauxhall Walk, London SE11 5HJ

2 4 6 8 10 9 7 5 3 1

This book has been typeset in Avenir

Printed in China

British Library Cataloguing in Publication Data:
a catalogue record for this book is available from the British Library

ISBN 978-1-5295-0443-9

www.walker.co.uk

Uh-oh!
Rabbit

WALKER BOOKS
AND SUBSIDIARIES

LONDON • BOSTON • SYDNEY • AUCKLAND

Jo Ham

Rabbit up

Uh-oh!

Rabbit down

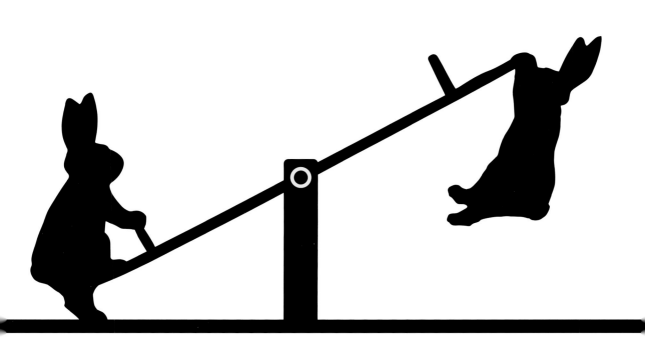

Rabbit up

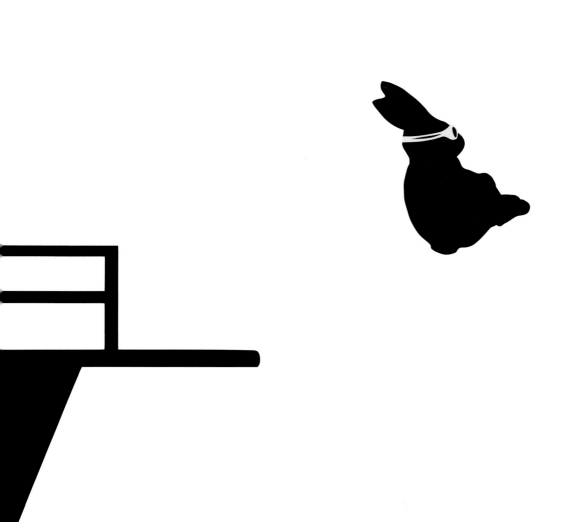

Uh-oh!

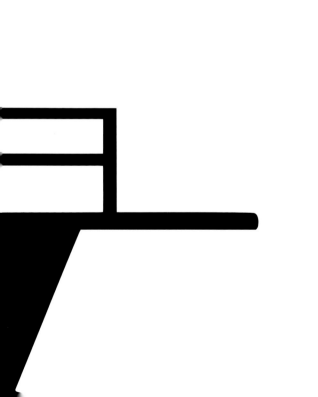

Rabbit down

Rabbit up

Uh-oh!

Rabbit down

Rabbit up

Uh-oh!

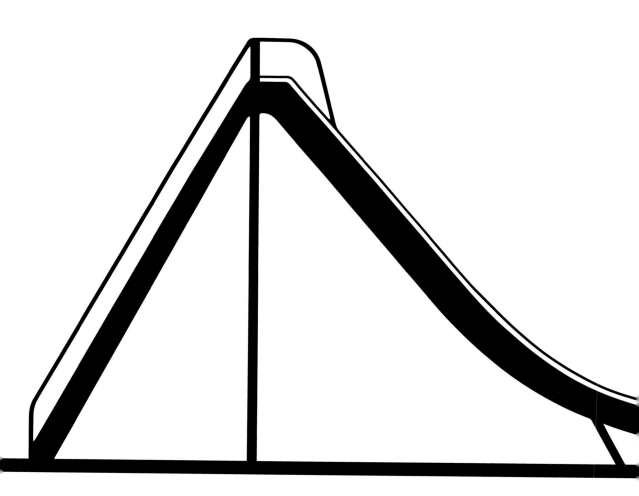

Rabbit UP!